Junior Tennis Excellence

Junior Tennis Excellence

Robert "Bob" Clauson

Library of Congress Control Number: 2012919146

ISBN:	Hardcover	978-1-4797-3229-6
	Softcover	978-1-4797-3228-9
	Ebook	978-1-4797-3230-2

Disclaimer
Unless otherwise stated, this book is a compilation of my opinions only. My opinions may or may not agree with other people's opinions on this book's subject matter. This book simply contains information as to how I see and teach the game of tennis and how very much it is similar to life itself.

Robert "Bob" Clauson
USPTA
Professional Tennis Instructor

This book was printed in the United States of America.

To order additional copies of this book, contact:
Xlibris Corporation
1-888-795-4274
www.Xlibris.com
Orders@Xlibris.com
119279

Contents

I am dedicating this book to my son, Adam R. Clauson, who has realized that he has a passion for teaching the game of tennis and has now embarked on a career of teaching and training junior tennis players in the Pacific Northwest.

Good luck and God speed your spirit, my son, and may you find as much everlasting joy in teaching the great game of tennis as I have enjoyed.

Have faith in yourself.

I love you.

Dad

A Note to Parents

This book on junior tennis speaks not only of my instruction and coaching methods of the game of tennis, but also of my philosophy on how the game of tennis is fundamental to life.

When a junior chooses to learn to become a competitive tennis player, I believe he has chosen something that is not only an extremely fulfilling venture in itself, but will also give them a leg up on life. Most all of the necessary elements to a successful life are found in the game of tennis.

Way before youngsters opt to play competitive tennis, the word "want" has become the most dominant word in their vocabulary, other than possibly the word "why." The more juniors achieve in tennis, the more they must exhibit an understanding of such virtues as responsibility, dependability, perseverance, and most of all, self-reliance. For all of these words to be put into play, the word **"want"** has to be involved. So if you place the words **I want to be** in front of each of aforementioned words, then the question arises—**how badly do they want to do this? What are they willing to sacrifice to get what they want? Just how big of a price are they willing to pay?**

The word "want" has a value . . . it seems to me that the **want in youngsters today has been diluted down so much that things that are received have almost no price attached to them at all.**

I often hear about youngsters having no self-esteem . . . so now we seem to be trying to find a way to help give them some self-esteem. **To me self-esteem cannot be given . . . it must be earned.** Tennis is all about the individual. And being independent. **This is why I have such a passion about the game of tennis. It is filled with hard work and self-sacrifice.** All preceded by the words **I want to . . . It is a choice, to want to be something special, to rise above, and to earn the self-esteem and pride that is associated with being an accomplished tennis player. It all starts with the word "want." It has to be something they want to do more than anything else.**

Acknowledgments

There are two people I would like to recognize as having a profound effect on my life as a tennis instructor and coach.

First, Mr. Vic Braden of the Vic Braden Tennis College in Coto de Caza, California.

I first met Vic about thirty-five years ago, at the Rancho Bernardo community tennis courts. It was about noon on a Saturday. I was returning from a golf game when I noticed a crowd gathering at the community center tennis courts. I parked and went to see what was happening. Vic Braden and a gentleman by the name of Tony Trabert were giving a tennis clinic to the residents of Rancho Bernardo. My intention was only to check out what was going on and then go on my way . . . But Mr. Braden was conducting a tennis clinic like only he can. The clinic lasted just a few hours; however, in that short period of time, I became a Vic Braden fan. I put away my golf clubs, bought a tennis racket, and began to sit in on as many of Vic's tennis college lectures as I could. It seemed as though I was following him everywhere he went, and believe me, he went to plenty of different places. I watched and listened as he would infect each and every student in his clinic . . . with his love and knowledge of the game. To this day, I have never met anyone who has such a passion for the game of tennis. I soon realized that I too had been infected with the Braden tennis virus. So I made a decision to completely change the direction of my life. I had to be realistic though . . . I knew that I was way too old to become a professional tennis player, so I decided to dedicate the rest of my life to becoming the very best professional tennis instructor I could possibly be.

Thank you, Mr. Vic Braden, for giving me the inspiration to do what I do . . . you showed me a path that would allow me to begin to fulfill a childhood dream—to become a coach and work with young people. Prior to this, I had been working for the sake of working, not really loving what I was doing. Even today as I grow deeper into my senior years, I still love to teach and coach tennis. It continues to this day, to be my great passion in life. Each day, I am still looking for a way to give a better lesson. How lucky I am to have met Mr. Vic Braden . . . thank you, my friend, for all the great memories.

Second, I want to say thank you to Mr. and Mrs. Elias Roditi, for entrusting me to be the guardian of their son, David Roditi. David moved from his home in Guadalajara, Mexico, to live and train with me in Southern California at the young age of thirteen years.

David spoiled me, in that I found out early in my coaching career what it was like to work with an extremely talented junior player who was driven to excel. He always wanted to be the best player on the court, no matter whom he was playing with. He had a passion for the game. As I look back on my years with David, I believe he taught me more than I taught him.

In my thirty plus years of coaching junior tennis players, I have never been on the court with someone who consistently exhibited such a true passion to excel at playing the game of tennis. From the get go, I believe that David knew inside of him that he not only could become a great champion of the game, but that he would become a great champion of the game. As for me today, he is a great champion of the game.

David achieved all-American honors at both San Clemente High School and Texas Christian University. He attained a world ATP doubles ranking of number 40. David also fulfilled a lifelong dream when he was invited to represent the country of Mexico as a member of their Davis cup tennis team. After his life on the professional tennis tour, David became the assistant coach for the University of Texas men's tennis team. He then became the assistant director of the St. Stephen's Episcopal School Tennis Academy in Austin, Texas, then he joined the USTA coaching staff at their training center in Carson, California. As of the writing of this book, David has been named the men's head tennis coach at his alma mater, the Texas Christian University in Fort Worth, Texas. How great is that? He has now transferred that same great passion he had as a player to coaching his beloved frogs.

Thank you, David, for sharing your young life with me and for being such an important part of my growth in life, both as a person and a tennis coach . . . you are the best . . . go frogs!

Purpose of This Book

The purpose of this book is to offer young tennis players information that **will give them pause to actually think about what it is they are trying to learn** . . . to understand that they must master all of the fundamentals of the game in order to excel at playing it . . . to keep it simple . . . that it all starts with a thought; how basic is that—that thoughts are the very beginning of doing or learning anything. My hope is that this book will inspire junior players . . . to play competitive tennis at the intercollegiate or even professional level . . . to become a tennis player, not just a person who plays tennis. My goal for this book is to accelerate the young players' learning curve. **Learning—it is life's food for success.**

Tennis has to be a way of life. It is a choice you make. If you do choose to play the game of tennis, give it your very best effort, hold nothing back, and commit to being the best player you can possibly be**. Please study this book. Don't just read it; make it your workbook,** underlining parts in the book and making notes as you see fit. I hope that you will keep it in your tennis bag and refer to it as often as necessary . . . even on change over in a match.

Tennis is all about self-motivation, discipline, responsibility, and perseverance . . . the rest of it is just plain hard work and practice. It is for those who can focus their thoughts quickly enough to give them an opportunity to succeed. Please notice that I said the word "opportunity."

There are **no guarantees of outcome in tennis or in life . . . no outside assistance. Nothing is really fair in tennis or in life; everything is earned . . . just you and the ball you wish to control, giving you the satisfaction and pride of accomplishment. No matter what you do in tennis or in life, you must understand that you are representing you, and the greatest part is that you get to choose both in tennis and in life what you want to be. Be prideful of your work so as to be an example for others to emulate.**

Give the game your very best effort every day, and it will reward you with a lifetime of enjoyment . . . and will allow doors to open for you in the future that might otherwise remain closed . . .

Passion

I begin this book with the word "passion." If your desire is to play high-level tennis, this is the one word that must be at the core of your inner being; it will enable you to dream your dream every day. You will find love in doing **the day-to-day work, and your sacrifices will become worth your investment**. Tennis excellence is impossible to achieve without passion. You must be willing to put in the extra time necessary to achieve the goals that you have set. To find this time, you will need to give up other things you might wish to do. The words sacrifice, discipline, dedication, and perseverance will become words to live by. If you have passion, your after-school hours and weekends will become committed to learning the game and playing competitive matches. Now sacrifice becomes an everyday event, giving up other so-called normal activities so that you can pursue your dream to play some "big tennis."

One of my favorite words in tennis and in life is the word "want." You may call it desire. If there is a formula for success, it might be that the amount of success achieved will be directly proportional to the amount of want supplied. How badly do you want something? What are you willing to give up to get what you want? Will you go after it? Everything has a price. What are you willing to pay? It is there for the taking, if you are willing to sacrifice things to get it, don't be detoured. Push your limits every day . . . make sure that you find out. Just how high is too high? How far is too far? How big is too big, and for sure, how tired is too tired? **Don't place any limitations on your abilities to learn and succeed**. You will find that most of the time, the person you see in the mirror is your biggest obstacle, and that person will be responsible for placing most of the limitations on your development as a tennis player. This same person can also be your best friend and greatest motivator . . . your pal . . . your buddy. Be good to you . . . say nice things to you . . . encourage you . . . let you know how proud you are of you. After all, you are one of a kind . . . forever and ever. No duplicates here . . . you are extra special. I dare you to go for greatness; very few people do. If you have true passion, you will find the word "fun" replacing the word "work" in your vocabulary. No matter what you choose to do in tennis or in life, if you have true passion for what it is you are doing, you will never work a day in your life. You will always have fun in doing it. **Let's go have some fun!**

Mental

If passion is the driving force behind being successful in playing the game of tennis, **then the mental aspect of the game is the governing or controlling aspect of the game**. There really is very little chance that you would be able to do much of anything on the tennis court, or in life for that matter, if you are unable to successfully control your thoughts. These thoughts are the nifty little things that tell you what to do and how to do it. Now all you have to do is be able control those thoughts so that you will make the correct positive choice as to what you want to take place. Pretty much all you do in tennis and in life will play out in your mind first, hence the often-used phrase . . . **the game is played between your ears.** It is often used because it's so very true. As I go forward in this book, I will use the word "visualize" many times over. **Make sure that you fully understand just how important that word is to the game of tennis. Without vision, there is only confusion and failure . . . be a master of what you think and you will have a chance to be a master of what you want to do.**

The words and thoughts that follow are meant for you to ponder. That is a word I learned when I moved to Texas . . . to think about . . . to use as tools to help you in your quest for tennis excellence. **It is important to understand that everything you do will start with a thought. Now, will that be a positive or a negative thought? You must make a choice. It will pretty**

much determine how you are going to learn to play the game.

Accentuate the positive, eliminate the negative, and don't mess with Mr. In Between . . . Those words are in a song that I learned as a teenager. That is some great advice. **I can, I will are positive statements . . . they stand alone. In other words, they are the truth. You don't have to think about them . . . they just are. For them to become negative, you have to choose to make them so. Can't and won't are unable to live without the positive words can and will, so that makes them untrue or false. If you understand this, you will see why what you choose to think about on the tennis court becomes so very important. Are your thoughts positive or negative?** I would ask you . . . how do you feel when your thoughts are positive? How do you feel when you are negative? Be aware of this difference in feelings . . . it is important to recognize what you feel when you are playing a match . . . knowing the difference will go a long way toward keeping you in the positive mode.

In tennis and in life, staying positive is mandatory. Mr. In Between is when you are in doubt or haven't made up your mind . . . Kind of like a purgatory . . . you really aren't sure which way you are going. If you have the will, you can develop the skill . . . **you would not have the desire to play the game of tennis if you didn't have the talent.** That is very important for you to know. It is a difficult game to play . . . **believe in yourself and in what you are doing. Go for what you want. Don't hold anything back . . . doubt and negativity invite failure. Your game will follow your thoughts**. In order for you to perform a shot successfully, you first have to be able to visualize it. It will always happen in your mind first. Visualization is so very necessary to give a great performance. I believe the following to be true. **You will win or lose in your mind first. You can't rise above what you think of yourself. You were not created to be average.**

Can you imagine jumping out of bed each day and proclaiming with great enthusiasm, "Hooray! Today I am going to be mediocre. I am going to be average. I am going to be content . . . I am going to be moderate." Those kind of words really have no place in the making of a champion or in the living of life. When describing Boris Becker's success, Jim Loehr, a noted PhD, said that **the very thing that brought Becker's greatness to the surface is potentially in all of us**. "We all have the capacity for greatness, passion, commitment, and purpose. It is the force and the direction of our energy that makes the impossible possible." These are great words for sure.

I had the opportunity to be teaching for a short time on the court next to a very inspirational coach by the name of Randy Snow, who has since passed away. As the writing of this book, Randy is being inducted into the tennis hall of fame . . . such a deserving young man. Randy was coaching wheel chair tennis at the St. Stephen's Episcopal School Tennis Academy in Austin, Texas, when he offered me a copy of his book **Not Far from Home**. There is a passage in the book that says, "God is not Glorified with mediocrity. I can do it because I am . . . be thankful you are alive . . . your tennis court will be your workshop . . . and your workshop will be your worship." These are some great words from an inspirational young man. I recommend strongly that you get a copy of Randy's book . . .

and you will know about thinking positively and overcoming adversity . . . about true passion. What a great inspiration he was to me. I knew him such a short time. But each time we were together, we were able to visit about tennis and life.

Please know that your mind is a very unique thing . . . it is always on duty. It never rests. As a result, your eyes are continually bringing information into your mind for you to have thoughts about . . . for example, you are playing a match on court number 3, but when you are not engaged in a point, you find yourself watching the match on court 4. **That is the ultimate in losing focus as to what you are trying to accomplish.** Don't let your eyes wander; if you do, they will just feed you erroneous information about something you should have absolutely no interest in. The match you are playing is your world. **Remember, much of it is played in your mind first . . . focus . . . focus . . . focus.**

Realize that you have only two choices in tennis and in life—one is to be positive and the other is to be negative. What possible good can come from being negative? Absolutely nothing!

Pressure, along with fear, faith, adversity, courage, and anger make up the six big words that will immensely affect your tennis career. There are so many tennis descriptions of the word "pressure." It may be the most widely used word in the game. I like to call it **the cooker**. This is where learning is accelerated. Graduate school so to speak . . . the cooker is a place you have to want to be in. It is a goal, a place you have earned . . . a victory of sorts . . . you know . . . you are 30-40 match point down, and you are serving . . . you are now in the cooker. **You can feel the pressure . . . know that when you are in the cooker, you have arrived . . . you have earned an opportunity to grow . . . to rise above. This is where progress is made . . . learning on steroids . . . this is where greatness lives . . . without pressure, you are never really involved in the match . . . you know . . . mediocre, and you have already determined that you don't want that. So love the moment . . . no safe zone in the cooker . . . now we play to win. This is your opportunity to grow.**

Fear . . . this word is not an option. If you are using it or even thinking about it on the tennis court, then stop it at once. Clean up your thoughts. **There are no real consequences if you miss a shot or lose a tough point**. Remember, this is a game you are playing . . . no one is in danger of losing a body part. **Fear lives only in**

your mind . . . it is a product of negativity . . . and you have already decided that you don't want any part of negativity. Fear of losing . . . fear of missing . . . fear of what your coach or your parents or your friends will say . . . when you put fear into tennis context, it sounds really silly. Believe me, you have nothing to fear on the tennis court, yet this four-letter word "fear" is so powerful when it gets into your mind, it can turn you to stone . . . absolutely frozen in time. All of a sudden, your mechanics don't work . . . and your mind goes nuts . . . and you are unable to think . . . like when you have a second serve on a big point and suddenly the service box looks half its size, and all you can visualize with your negative mind-set is a double fault. Guess what happens . . . you proceed to double-fault . . . remember, it happens in your mind first. When fear shows up, think positively. Talk to it under your breath, but sort of out loud so you hear what you are saying. Let it know that you are in charge. Have faith, and know that you have done the work necessary to get the job done . . . you have done the work, haven't you?

You will play your best when you have nothing to fear. Without fear, you can find rhythm and confidence. These two words seem to beget each other . . . the more rhythm you have, the more confidence you have; and the more confidence you have, the more rhythm you have. Pretty soon the ball looks very large, and you can do anything you want with it . . . this aptly is called **being in the zone**. You actually get lost in what you are doing, and nothing else exists anywhere around you. **You are in your element. Your mind and your body are one . . .**

Faith . . . is a word often used when referring to what you believe to be true. You have faith that you can get it done because you know that you have put in all of the work and sacrifice necessary to do the job . . . you have mastered your homework . . . the more prepared you are, the more faith will play a large role in your performance. Now you can truly believe in yourself, so you can be positive about the outcome . . . it is often said according to your faith . . . so will it be **. . . so have faith in yourself. Believe in yourself. If you don't believe in you, why should anyone else believe in you?**

Adversity . . . this word in many respects goes hand in hand with pressure. Each level of success has its own demons to deal with . . . . adversity is meant to challenge you. It will help to accelerate your growth or slow your growth . . . depending on how you handle the task at hand. **Beyond the word "adversity" lies the word "opportunity"** . . . and opportunities are what you are looking to find, for without an opportunity, how can you possibly improve? There are no guarantees of outcomes, only opportunities to affect the outcome.

Courage . . . this word is necessary to deal with adversity and pressure. **Great achievement comes when you have the courage to dare to risk failure, often several times during a match. The battle between adversity and courage is an ongoing test. You must have faith in your ability to perform**. This is a fact of both tennis and life. As you have already probably learned, you will fail many more times than you succeed. So be continually seeking opportunities to advance your skills; don't blow an opportunity by wimping out or playing safe.

In both of these instances, you learn absolutely nothing. It is very important for you to understand that a whole bunch of learning takes place when you risk failure. Even though you do fail, you succeed because you took a risk . . . you went for it . . . no risk, no reward. So be positive, go forward, and take the risk. You might just make it . . . and if not this time, then next time. Keep on keeping on. **Be a doer of things, even though you might make a mistake. It is okay because doers make mistakes**. Don't fear mistakes by playing safe. Go for it. It is how you handle those mistakes that will determine your success. Mistakes are actual building blocks for success. Fear works exactly like faith. **You will get what you believe you will get** . . . learn from your mistakes. If you ever think that you are through learning, then you are really through. **Real losers are too afraid to take a**

risk, so they never even try to win. They always want to play safe and then lose. Have you ever noticed how you begin to feel when you get close to winning versus how you feel when you get close to losing? Don't get comfortable giving in to safe. **Safe is negative; take the risk and give yourself a chance to win.** Remember the word "mediocrity"? This is where mediocrity lives—in the safe zone . . . in the land of the uncommitted. Courage will give you the necessary energy to prevail over fear. **Courage is the one word that sets you apart . . . the wanting to excel . . . and you are willing to risk failure to get what it is that you want. Make your mark.**

Anger . . . this word is so powerful it overwhelms any situation. Nothing else can exist when anger enters the conversation . . . reason leaves immediately . . . rationality goes out of the window for sure. Losing control of your emotions will virtually guarantee that you will lose control of your motions. Don't let anger enter into your mind-set. **Emotional balance is mandatory for physical balance to be maintained . . .** if anger enters your match, take it over to the corner of the court and talk to it . . . get it all cleaned out; don't leave any residue. Regain your focus of thought; make sure all of the anger is gone before you continue to play. **Remember, you and only you should be affecting your thoughts . . . the anger started with a thought, and you chose to be negative or in this case—angry, so get rid of it with a thought. Keep your thoughts positive**. You are all alone on the court, and your best friend or your worst enemy happens to be wearing your shoes . . . no negativity allowed . . . **positive thinking is mandatory. If you are a player who**

has a tendency to lose his temper, you might consider going to a mirror before you go on the court and get a good look at your partner for the match. Give yourself a high five and talk to yourself positively. In doubles, can you imagine your partner getting mad at you and losing his temper during the match? Just how long do you think that would work out? Keep your mind clean of negativity. Give yourself a lot of atta boys. Be respectful of both you and the game of tennis. On and off the court, be a good role model for others to emulate. If you know that anger and reason can't coexist, then don't tolerate allowing anger to enter your thought process. Remember, everything starts with a thought, so control your thoughts. Being mentally tough must be practiced too. It takes work and patience to learn to be in control of what you are thinking. It is sometimes called being in focus. Don't let anything detour you from giving a great performance. Be in charge of your thoughts, and that will put you in charge of you. Remember, you must be in charge of you in order for you to be in charge of the ball, and that is the true objective in the game—to control the ball and get it to work for you and to do what you want it to do. Keep working every day to be the best you can be. **Have great expectations . . . expect to win.**

The following is a poem that was given to me by my dad. **It was authored by Larry Bielat; it can be found in the book** Winning Words of Champions.

Believe in yourself! Believe you were made
To do any task without calling for aid
Believe, without growing too scornfully proud
That you, as the greatest and least are endowed.
A mind to do thinking, two hands and two eyes
Are all the equipment God gives to the wise.

Believe in yourself! You're divinely designed
And perfectly made for the work of mankind.
This truth you must cling to through danger and pain.
The heights man has reached you can also attain.
Believe to the very last hour, for it's true,
That whatever you will, you have been gifted to do.

Believe in yourself! And step out unafraid,
By misgivings and doubt be easily swayed.
You've the right to succeed; the precision of skill
Which betokens the great you can earn if you will!
The wisdom of ages is yours if you'll read, but you've got to believe in yourself to succeed.

Somehow this man captured the true understanding of just how each of us is an entity unto ourselves. And what a powerful force our mind is. Be positive. Your accomplishments in tennis and in life will be as you choose them to be.

The one thing that sets you apart from others is your mind and how you think. Be aware of what you are thinking; positive thoughts rule!

Physical Balance

As important as physical balance is, it is totally controlled by your emotional balance. The way I see these two factors is if you can control your emotions, then you have the opportunity to control your motions or your physical balance. How very important that little **e** is located in front of the word "motions." Understanding this fact, I will continue with some words about physical balance on the tennis court. Remember, your thoughts are going to give your body assignments to perform in a balanced manner. First and foremost, move about the court in the ready position with small quick steps, keeping your knees consistently flexed with your heels slightly off the ground. This will help you keep your head quiet for all of the shots you may make during a match. Your head must not be moving up and down, like a cork in the ocean, so that you will be able to keep your eyes lower and more aligned with the level of the ball. Of all the professional players I have ever watched, I believe that Jimmy Connors stayed in this position better than any other player, but he also probably hit the ball flatter than anyone else. This will certainly make focusing on the ball a lot easier. Pulling your head out of the shot, so as not to finish watching the ball, is probably in the top three reasons why you miss a shot. Even among today's touring pros. **Everybody wants to see how they are doing, and as a result, they get to see a loser**. The head must remain perfectly still until you have finished your shot on balance. I use the analogy that the head is a camera, and pictures will be blurred if your head is bouncing around. The eyes are the lenses, so they alone can move about to track the ball. The more quiet your head remains, the fewer variables you will have. Thereby you will be able to exhibit a lot more consistency in your motions, and a **word you want to exhibit in a tennis match is consistency.**

As you move about the court, keep your head between your feet. I regard your head as your center of balance. If you move your head to the right, outside of your right foot, you will be off-balance to the right; that is why in today's tennis, many shots are hit with an open stance for both forehands and backhands. Now the head is pretty much over the hitting foot but still not outside of the hitting foot. This makes the hitting foot also the weight-bearing foot, and good players are able to reach further out to the side to get wide balls, without losing position, which enables them to return quickly back into the court with a simple crossover step.

When a player I am coaching goes out for their match, my first bit of advice is **to stay low and keep your head still**. If you can remember this until it becomes a way of life in a tennis match, you will go a long ways toward becoming a pretty good tennis player.

Serve

There is absolutely no reason whatsoever for a tennis player to have a bad serve. It is the one shot that you are able to completely control; you even get to hold the ball. How great is that? It is the most important shot in the game; it is a confidence builder. Nothing happens until you serve the ball successfully into your opponent's service box. It is the first building block of a point—the shot that all other shots depend on; there can't be any excuses here, just you and the ball. The serve should not be just a way to start the point, you need to make aces . . . free poin**ts. It is somewhat**

okay to have a couple of double faults if you are making more aces than double faults, But you will never make aces if you aren't trying to make them. So make sure that you learn to hit the best possible serve you can both first and second serve; both of these should be weapons. Why is the second serve more important than the first serve? Because there isn't a third serve. I have often heard it said that **you are as good as your second serve**. I believe that to be very true; be sure and practice serving until you can master both first and second serve. I mean, until you can do them in the dark . . . until you have no doubt about your ability to execute the serve of your choice on command. As for me, I believe that the only difference between a first serve and a second serve is that one comes before the other. There are many times that you will want to hit a so-called second serve first, in order to keep your opponent off-balance. **So a second serve really only states that you have just missed your first serve**, and this is your last chance. Don't you hate to double-fault? Don't even have that negative thought because serving will have a lot to do with your winning or losing matches. The serve is the same as a drive in golf . . . try to win a golf match if your drive goes out of bounds or into the woods every time you have to drive the ball. All of a sudden you have no chance. To become a great tennis player, it is mandatory that you have a great first and second serve. Placement is more important than power, but if you can develop both, you are definitely "standing in some tall cotton." Learn how to serve the ball into the service box, much like a baseball player pitches a baseball to different spots in the strike one . . . move it around.

If you're right handed, learn to hit a topspin kicker to the add court and slice side spin to the deuce court . . . the opposite if you are a lefty. There is very little I can say about the mechanics of the serve, as there are so many different types of serves. I can however say that I believe your serve will be as good as your leg strength. Don't jump and then hit the ball; be hitting the ball as you are rising up so that you make contact at the peak of your jump, snapping your wrist forward, at the same time your thumb is rotating forward, **keeping your head up past your contact point**. Try to watch the racket hit up and over the ball; make sure that your body weight lands at least one foot inside the court on your lead foot on balance with your back foot raised high behind you. Again, much like a pitcher in baseball the visual of the pitchers finish will help you understand how you need to finish; it is important to keep your wrist very flexible, almost loose . . . the wrist snap is a necessity. You can even practice serving by holding your racket up and using only your wrist to snap the ball into the service box. Doing this motion often will help strengthen your wrist.

The ball toss . . . I am not fond of the word "toss." To me, you toss salads and frisbees . . . not tennis balls. This part of the serve is definitely the most important because it begins the entire service motion; you can't afford to have variables here or you will forever remain inconsistent with your placement of the ball, and an inconsistent beginning pretty much guarantees an inconsistent serve. Again, using the golfer analogy, imagine the golfer teeing his ball up in a different place every time he hits his drive. Again . . . no chance for consistency.

To begin your service motion, make sure that your lead shoulder is pointed toward the target you wish to hit and your chin resting against it. Then look at the spot or target in their service box you want the ball to hit; from there, lift your eyes directly up and keep them up until well after the hit. Visualization is so very important. When you begin to lift the ball up into position to hit, it should be located at about one o'clock and one foot inside the court. See it in your mind first Lifting the ball upward in one continuous motion by pushing your hips and knees forward, raising your heels slightly off the ground and lifting arm up so as to bring your ball-lifting shoulder higher than your hitting shoulder, **the trophy pose,** will commit you to hit up into the ball, landing on your lead foot about one foot into the court. The service motion must be one continuous motion, no stopping. You have to have a rhythm to perform a serve correctly . . . and for there to be rhythm, there can be no stopping and starting . . . I hope you remember learning about inertia in school—a body in motion wants to stay in motion. As you are preparing to hit the serve, you should be breathing in so as to exhale on impacting the ball; **this breathing rhythm takes place pretty much on all tennis shots. Every time you strike a ball, it is air in for preparation and air out at contact . . . players exaggerate this exhaling with sound by grunting, humming, or even yelling so as to make sure that they are contracting their abdominal muscles at the instant ball contact is made.** I do believe that this action helps a players to have all of their attention focused on the instant that the racket meets the ball.

Master a topspin kick serve into the backhand side of the returner. And a slicespin serve that takes the returner off the court on the forehand side. For those of you who wish to work on a better service motion, practice throwing a small football, getting it to have a tight spiral. Make sure that you lead with your throwing elbow going forward followed by snapping your wrist and thumb forward and throwing the football up so that it has an arc as it travels through the air.

Technique is everything; master your motion. Serving is an art form; you must practice your serve endlessly, every day if possible. To me, it is so very necessary to **always use targets when you are practicing your serve. It will help to train your mind to be specific. You must be specific as to where the ball lands. I mean be exact.**

A note to the young ladies about the serve. At great personal risk with the political correct crowd, I must make note of the fact that young ladies have a more difficult time learning a good service motion than do boys. But there is a very good reason for this—it is because when boys are very young, they are already throwing things about. So they get a lot of repetitions in the throwing motion. That is a good way to practice learning a good service motion—just lift the ball up and throw the racket at the ball, without letting go of the racket. You will be surprised as to how quickly you will begin to have a good service motion. Quality women's tennis requires a serve of 85 miles per hour plus.

If you can, get a radar gun and practice your serve until you are able to reach the 85 mph goal. Now you can compete with yourself to increase your speed over time. Just getting the ball in and starting the point is no longer acceptable. You have got to be able to nail your serve . . . **To really increase your chances of winning matches, master the kick serve on your second serve**. Good returners are teeing off on many of the slow second serves in women's tennis. Remember, if you can always hold your serve, it will be tough to lose; for someone to use as an example of a great server, watch Serena Williams. I do believe that she has the best serve in women's tennis and probably the best ever in women's tennis with the possible exception of Martina Navratilova. For a kicker serve, watch Sam Stosar of Australia. Good luck and good serving! Practice . . . practice . . . practice.

Return of Serve

Return of serve is the second most important shot in the **game. If you aren't a great server, you better be a great returner of serve or your matches are going to be really short.** Nothing happens unless you get the ball back into play preferably to a spot deep to the baseline of the server's court; depth of a return is a must . . . **short returns are generally very short points . . . and guess what, you generally lose them**. Don't just get good at the shot. Master it. Very few players practice this shot enough. Andre Agassi seems to me to be an absolute artist at the service return, always applying pressure to the server. Watch his eyes, how totally focused they are, almost like a mongoose watching a cobra waiting for his chance to strike. The rest of the point will depend on you having a really terrific return of serve. **You want your opponents shot back to you, after your return, to be an opportunity shot. Where you go on the offense and try to close out the point. If you can't break your opponent's serve, you really have no chance of winning. Make sure that you are not backing up when you are retuning serve. If you are, you are already on your heels and in a negative mind-set, and your chance of a good return is substantially reduced and you are just playing it safe and trying to get the ball back into play is giving your opponent a slower ball to act on in an offensive manner. Constantly practice going forward to hit on all of your returns . . . be in charge of the ball.**

When you are waiting for your opponent to serve, take some practice swings. Move about, forward to the baseline then back again, like Agassi if you will. He would be constantly moving up and back on the baseline. Then get into the ready position with your legs out wide. But keep your feet gently moving like an idling engine in a car. Then when the ball is served to you, put yourself in gear and go after the ball. Remember, forward gear please, not reverse.

It is difficult to describe the shot, suffice to say, keep it simple. **Little or no backswing, get your feet moving forward and make a split step**, rotating your shoulders either right or left, then hitting the ball early, out in front and moving through the ball, all the while keeping your head rock still behind the racket head. Above all, have a target on the court you want to hit. **Remember, if you aim at nothing, you**

will surely hit it. Think!! Visualize where you want the ball to go . . . having targets on returns will keep you **focused**.

Learn a slice return off both sides . . . learn a lob return for doubles play. This shot is not often used, but the great players can make it. That is one of the things that makes them great players. It wakes up your opponent's net person, especially if they are playing too tight on the net.

Be aggressive on returns, **especially on your opponent's second serves. These are opportunities to score. Don't give your opponent any free second serves. Put some doubt in their mind, even if you miss. Your opponent will take note, and it may make for some nervousness on the server's part . . . go for a few winners. Make them doubt their**

ability to serve. The more success you have on your returns, the more they will press and start to double-fault.

Returning from inside the baseline will definitely make your opponent feel your presence.

If they have a big serve, then slice or chip or even block the ball back into to play. Do whatever it takes to get into the point . . . learn all of these shots on returning the ball. At the beginning of a match, sometimes it is a good idea to start a little deeper behind the baseline to give yourself a little more time to adjust to the speed of your opponent's serve. You know, check it out. Going too far back however will increase the angles that you will have to contend with. Keep trying to apply pressure by going forward to contact the ball. Most of the time, the second serve will be shorter in the box and slower. Now you can be acting on the ball instead of reacting. Make them press so they try to outhit their ability. You certainly want to give them every opportunity to miss. Now the double faults might start to happen . . . pressure, pressure, apply the pressure. They might not like the cooker.

When your opponent is getting ready to serve, let your eyes focus on your service line. That is where the ball will be landing, then track your eyes up to where the server will make contact with the ball. Move your eyes up and down between these two places. This way you will be able to pick up the ball as it enters your service box quicker so you can be a bit earlier in hitting your returns. Give your opponent reason to fear your return. A return ace counts just as much as a service ace. Free points! And some great postmatch conversation. Be ready for your return with a forehand grip until your opponent can prove to you, they can consistently hit to your backhand; this should make it easier to hit inside out returns from the add court. Plus your forehand is generally a stronger and more versatile shot. If the server keeps serving to the wide side, move over a bit. Don't just let him keep on doing it.

Ground Strokes

In discussing ground stroke grips, I tread lightly, as grips used may vary from player to player. I like to see a junior begin with a semi-western forehand grip. A continental grip for the serve, slice, volley, and overhead. For the backhand, I teach a grip where the student has the option later to switch easily from a two-handed backhand to a one-handed backhand, so the dominant hand is a little more left of continental.

Forehands

Variables . . . there are two types of variables: (1) those that come from within you and you are able to control, i.e., your strokes, and (2) those that come from your environment and you are unable to control, i.e., the sun, the wind, etc. As I pass on information about strokes, I will use the word "variables" often. **Your inability to control your own controllable variables will reduce drastically your physical ability to play championship level tennis . . . much the same as negativity will reduce your mental ability to play championship level tennis. Wherever you can, keep the negative motion required to get the job done to a minimum. By negative motion, I mean backswing. Remember, you are trying to keep the actual striking of the**

ball (the hitting zone) to be consistently the same, so shorten the backswing distance your racket has to travel before entering the hitting zone . . . work on simplicity or brevity if you will . . . keeping things simple will allow you to become more consistent more quickly, and a major goal to becoming a great tennis player is certainly consistency.

Generally speaking, **the least amount of negative motion, backswing, will make the least amount of mistakes, so keep your backswings short. Forward motion is positive motion, and backward motion is negative motion. The same is true if you are physically going forward toward the court or backward away from the court.**

I have heard it said that if you have a great serve and a great forehand, you can win a lot of matches. This is quite true. I would argue however, **if you are able to execute all of the shots in the game, you have a much greater chance to be a great player,** not just win some matches. After watching and studying Mr. Roger Federer, I don't believe there is a shot he can't execute almost at will. He has surely set the excellence bar very high.

It is difficult for me to describe a forehand, however, I would offer these suggestions: be sitting not only when you are hitting but all during the point and stay there for the duration of each and every shot in the entire match. Bending your knees sounds so very simple, yet so few players do it at all. I can remember Vic Braden telling me the story of a Davis cup match where one of the players was not doing so well, so the coach called his player over and whispered some advice in the player's ear. Vic was sure it was something really brilliant, so Vic asked the coach what advice did he give his player. The coach simply said, “Bend your knees and watch the ball.” How simple—two of the most fundamental lessons in tennis. Learn to keep your motion simple. I mean really simple. Have a semiopen stance, with your wrist cocked up. Turn your lead shoulder until it touches your chin with your arm out away from your body. Your weight should be loaded onto outside foot, and your racket hand should be held out away from your body and aligned with your hip and shoulder. Your wrist should still be cocked up. Dropping the racket head down below the flight of the ball, begin by pulling the butt of the racket up toward the ball, pushing your weight off the right foot up into the contact point. Rolling your racket head over the ball finishing on balance with your weight completely transferred to your left foot with your hitting shoulder reaching your chin while keeping your head so very still during the actual hit. The finish may be the most important part of the swing, so make sure that you exaggerate it finishing past where you made contact with the ball; a great finish presupposes a great beginning; however, you can have a great beginning without ever finishing. In teaching forehands, I ask the player to say the word finish out loud, elongating the word "finishhhhhhhhh." Just because you start something doesn't mean that you will finish what you started. Visualize what you want to look like when you finish your shot. Remember, **the farther back you take your racket, the deeper you are going into negative territory. Nothing good happens behind you. Too big of a backswing equals more variables, thus requiring more timing, giving you more inconsistency.**

Make sure that your racket head is speeding up as it rolls over the ball through the hitting zone, thereby increasing the speed of the topspin on the ball this will make sure that the ball is attacking the ground, which will create a good jump to the ball, causing it to rise up more quickly. The more perpendicular the bounce, the more difficult it is for your opponent to hit. I believe that Rafa Nadal has the most violent topspin in tennis, thus creating a huge kicking ball that is going aggressively up and out so quickly that it doesn't just rise up from the court, it explodes up. If I would describe Rafa's forehand, it has almost no backswing at all. In fact, his racket goes up, with his wrist severely cocked up, then down and back up . . . not so much back and forth. Thus, creating heavy topspin . . . sometimes Nadal's forehand actually finishes on the same side of his body high above his head. This allows him to hit with a wide open stance and be somewhat late on the hit; some are calling this type of forehand a buggy whip motion. More players are beginning to learn this shot and use it as another way to hit a forehand. It does gives a great spin to the ball and it will help you become more consistent. However, I don't believe this type of shot should replace the standard open stance forehand that rolls over the ball and finishes well to the other side of the player. A spinning ball is a ball that is working for you, one that you have under control. Make sure that you are able execute a wide open forehand stance when you are moving quickly to the wide side of the court. If this is done properly, you will find that sometimes you will make contact while you are in the air, finishing well past where you made contact with the ball, **again, keeping your**

head still during contact is mandatory. This is true of all shots. I believe this requirement is maybe the most important thing you need to master. Practice it until it is automatically you. It will go a long ways toward developing you into a top-level tennis player. Watch Federer, Tiger Woods, Gary Jeter. **They all meet the ball with their head completely quiet and locked in behind the ball at impact every time, not every other time or once in a while, but every time, and they keep it there until well after impact.** Your head is like a camera, and your eyes are the lens. You can't move the camera while you are taking a picture or you will have a blurry photo; plus if your head moves, it will change your core center of balance while you are hitting, causing you to either pull off the ball or be late and have your weight ahead of the hit, creating a huge variable in your entire motion and **you will never be consistent. Remember, to be consistent, you must do the exact same thing, the exact same way consistently. Every time. No variables. Master your motion. You must be able to control** both ends of your body, head, and feet. What happens to your strokes will totally depend on how well you can discipline the top and bottom of your body to be totally under control. After you have mastered the spinning ball and you have the confidence of consistency, then work on hitting a flatter ball, a more driving ball. By moving your hitting shoulder through and out rather than up the ball, make sure this ball is high enough above the net to drive. When stepping in to hit this type of ball, make sure that you are stepping as you are hitting Your hitting foot should land heel first just before contact. This allows your weight to go out onto the ball with a smooth rhythmical motion finishing with a complete and exaggerated shoulder follow-through. **Practice each of your ground stroke motions in front of a mirror**. It is important that you see what you look like. Not just on film, but as you actually make the motion. Mirrors are a big deal . . . use one! It is a great way to perfect a motion that you like. Do it often! As a guide to the forehand motion, if you wish to have a loop take away, then take the racket back not higher than your eyes (eye high). This way your hands stay well in the center of the motion. If your hands are going back eye high, your loop is unmanageable because your hands have become the circumference of the circle instead of your racket. Keep your loop small and efficient; big motions equal big mistakes. Some twenty years ago when I was teaching in Northern California, I began using the phrase

turn a doorknob with your hitting hand when executing the forehand. This will help keep your hand to be the center of the loop and not the circumference, and it will help to accelerate your racket head speed. **Don't be late; accelerate the racket head through the ball.**

Two-handed backhand

As in all ground strokes, make sure that you are sitting to hit and your knees are flexed. Turn your lead shoulder until it touches your chin, letting your hands drop down to be aligned with your hip. Now rotate your hips . . . keeping your arm long, showing the butt of the racket to the approaching ball, allowing your racket to brush up the bottom of the ball, finishing with both elbows high and your back shoulder up underneath your chin, making sure that your head is completely still and behind the contact point for the duration of the shot.

Again, exaggerate your follow-through motion with a fully rotated follow-through, finishing well past where you made contact with the ball. If the thumb on your left hand is pointing to your right ear, you have made a pretty complete follow-through . . . be able to hit this shot with a wide open stance and still finish past where you hit the ball. If this is done correctly, you may again find that you are actually making contact while you are in the air . . . finishing to the side well past your contact point. When you are able to get your feet organized to the point where you are behind the ball, then this is an opportunity to fully put your weight up onto the ball and hit a more penetrating shot, putting your opponent in trouble or even hitting an outright winner. **Remember, with most any ground stroke, if you have complete physical balance and the ball is in front of you, attack the ball, do something with it, be aggressive. Make something happen. Always be looking for an opening to be aggressive and go on the attack. Be thinking positively, no hesitation, rip it!**

One-handed backhand

Once again, sit to hit. Keep your knees flexed, staying low. Turn your lead shoulder taking the racket back with your off hand, which should be located on the throat of the racket. Make sure that the back of your lead shoulder sees the ball. This makes sure that you have a complete shoulder turn; your lead shoulder should be touching your chin. When you begin your forward motion, make sure that you are separating your hitting hand and your off hand at the same time in equal and opposite directions. At the same speed, forming the letter T with your arms. This will ensure that you stay on balance; for every action, there is an equal and opposite reaction. You may have learned that in school. Your racket should again be traveling with the butt of the racket being pulled toward the ball, brushing up from below the ball to make contact, allowing your finish to be with your racket head high above your head. This will allow you to place a great amount of spin and control on the ball . . .

Your contact point should be well in front of you so that your head can be in a position to see back through the strings. Your head must again be stone-still until the racket is high above your head. I believe that Roger Federer has the best one-handed backhand I have ever seen; his motion is so very precise, smooth and simple, variables are almost nonexistent. **His head never moves.** If you want a great "onie," copy Federer. Oh, by the way, his forehand is pretty good too, as are all of his shots. To my way of thinking, he is the most complete player there is or ever was, both on and off the court. What a great worldwide ambassador for the game of tennis!

Slices

To play tennis at the collegiate level, you must be able to execute both forehand and backhand slices perfectly Using about a forty-five-degree open face racket for both sides, will put a reverse spin on the ball, making the ball stay lower, causing your opponent to change their rhythm, keeping them off-balance. It is the prevolley shot, if there is such a thing, an approach shot that will allow you to go toward the net with good balance and rhythm. This will allow you to go directly into the volley position, because the racket is already in front of you when you finish your slicing motion, allowing for a smooth rhythmical transition into the court. But slicing is also just a different kind of ground stroke because you won't always be going into the court. You may choose to stay back and just change the spin on the ball so that your opponent will be surprised by the change in the bounce and cause them to mistime their shot. When slicing the ball, be sure and use a continual grip so that your palm and the racket face agree. **In order to be able to serve and volley effectively, you must master the slice**

off both sides when you are going deeper into the court.

Backhand slice . . . even though there are mostly two-handed backhands in junior tennis, I feel it is important that you take whatever time is necessary to learn how to execute a one-handed backhand slice. It is a much more efficient shot, plus it is easier to use and remain on balance, whether going into the court or staying back. Stay low with your knees flexed, completely turn your lead shoulder by pulling the racket back with your off hand, which should be holding the throat of the racket.

Take the racket back until your lead shoulder is touching your chin, keeping the racket face open to about forty-five degrees. Begin your hitting motion by pulling the butt of the racket through and under the ball following through so that your racket head finishes slight above your contact point, to form sort of a saucer motion. It is important to note that you should have your wrist kept extremely firm during this shot. No loose wrists or the racket head will fall away from the shot at contact. The moment you begin to pull the racket forward toward the ball, take your off arm back at the same speed as your hitting arm is going forward again forming the letter T with your arms. The back arm becomes a governor or a controller of your shoulders, keeping them sideways for the duration of the shot, enabling you to be able to maintain perfect balance. Again, for every action, there is an equal and opposite reaction. It certainly applies for the backhand slice. The length of your finish will vary as to the type of slice you are making. This is a shot you should practice over and over . . . you must be able to execute this shot at will and do it easily. Be able to hit this shot with both a closed and open stance . . . when executing this type of shot from the baseline be stepping as you are hitting and keep your weight forward almost leaning on the ball. When using the shot as an approach shot going into the court, bring your back foot in behind your lead foot so that you are making a reverse cross step so as to keep you sideways throughout the entire shot. Your back foot should be moving behind at the same time as your off arm is going back again making a T on the move. As a final point, remember to keep your head stone-still and have your contact point so that you head is just behind the racket head at impact. Keep it there until the shot is completely finished. A word of caution to the one-handed backhand players about the backhand slice being used as a ground stroke. Get really good at it, but don't fall in love with it so much that you start to use it in place of your lifting backhand. This does happen, and then you get to the point where you lose confidence in your topspin "onie."

Forehand slice . . . stay low and flex your knees. The forehand slice is more like a volley, because there is no need for very much of a backswing. You are basically placing the racket head a short distance in back of the oncoming ball at about forty-five degrees with your elbows pointing slightly down and outward, and your wrist firmly cocked up. The forehand slice is not used as much as the backhand slice, especially from the backcourt. However, it still can be an effective tool to use from the backcourt, especially when you want to change the spin on the ball as a method of forcing your opponent to change their rhythm . . . kind of a changeup if you will . . . a surprise. The forehand slice is certainly a valuable tool when it is used as an approach shot to go into the court to volley and finish off a point. Make sure that your follow-through is well past the contact point so that you are able to get your approach shot deep, preferably into the backhand court. I want to emphasize the word "deep" because a short approach shot is pretty much a suicide note. The point is over, and you lose, as with all shots, depth is so very important. Also, when going into the court you don't necessarily have to bring your back foot in behind as you did in the backhand slice, but sometimes you may wish to do so, to make sure that you don't pull the shot off line. When learning or practicing these two shots, do them together, alternating between forehand and backhand from just behind the service line, combining the necessary footwork to execute the shots, each time stepping into the ball you are hitting and finishing past each hit point, then backing up to come forward to do it again. It is important to be going up and back for this exercise, not just side to side.

Swinging forehand and backhand volleys

This type of shot has become a weapon to use when the ball is hanging in the air about midcourt. By hitting the ball out of the air in the same manner as a ground stroke, namely with lots of topspin **you are now able to hit an aggressive attacking ball for a winner rather that an approach shot followed by a volley**. This shot requires that the ball you are hitting to be either coming toward you slowly enough out of the air, or the ball has bounced midcourt in a somewhat perpendicular manner and the ball sits so that you are able to load up your weight and push off onto the ball. Practice these shots daily by doing them one after the other having a feeder place in the air for you. Try and do about ten in a row. You will learn the shot plus you will get stronger, as it is a good strength drill. Know this shot; it is a must for today tennis game.

Volleys

The volley shot is so very important for you to master.

It is a major part of today's winning tennis strategy.

You have to be able to close points out from the net.

Again, make sure your knees are flexed and they remain so for the duration of the point.

Using a continental grip, keep both Hands forward, with your elbows pointed slightly outward and well in front of you. This will enable you to be taking the racket directly to the ball with no backswing on either forehand or backhand. For the forehand volley, keep your wrist cocked up and go to the ball as if you were going to catch it, then push your racket through the ball. **Have someone throw some balls to you so you can practice the catching motion, and you will quickly see how naturally your hand goes to get the ball. The ball does not come to you.**

This is a big deal. Make sure you are leading with the bottom edge of the racket, and for sure, be stepping through the ball as you are hitting. For backhand volleys you again lead with the bottom edge of the racket with your wrist cocked up. **Being able to execute a backhand**

volley with no backswing requires a huge amount of self-control. The motion should be all forward, punching the racket through and stepping through the hit almost at the same time. The off hand again goes in the opposite direction to form the letter T with your arms. This is much like the one-hand backhand slice.

Without great footwork, there is no volley shot; you really do volley with your feet. Keep them moving. No loitering on the tennis court.

Also remember never to stop to hit a volley. Always hit through the spot where you make the contact. Make sure that you bend your knees lower to get a low volley; don't just drop your racket head.

When practicing volleys, do it from the serve line with targets deep in the corners of the court. Your first volley must get deep; if it is short, you are again looking at a second place finish on this particular point. Also try to do some volley drills where you hit the first volley from the serve line, and then close for a put-a-way volley. Try to always practice volleying in sequence, and for sure, practice them often. Make yourself a promise that you will learn to be a great serve and volleyer. Use this strategy in every match you play.

Overheads . . . . Good footwork is absolutely an essential requirement to execute a good shot. If there is one shot where this footwork thing becomes mandatory, it is the overhead. It is nearly impossible to hit a good overhead without the proper footwork. Get your feet organized so as to get you into position under the ball on balance to hit the overhead. Guess what shot I believe is the most underpracticed shot in junior tennis? You are right—the overhead. The second your opponent sends up a lob, you have to make a decision. Is it deep enough where you have to turn and run, or is it a little short, and you can get to it with a few simple crossover steps. **First, the short lob.** Turn your shoulders immediately raising both arms up . . . with the hitting arm holding the racket so that your elbow is up and pointing toward the back fence, and your racket head is behind your head with the edge of the racket pointing down. Try and hold this position while you are making the necessary crossover steps to put you in position to make the shot. As the ball descends, get your weight onto your back foot so that you can push yourself up. Be reaching up for the ball with your off hand as the ball is descending. **Don't let the ball fall down on you. You make sure you are going up to get the**

ball. Now, time your hit up into the ball so that you are basically hitting a serve with a good-wrist snap . . . pronating your thumb forward as your wrist is snapping. Many times you will find that making a scissor kick in the air will allow you to maintain your balance and be ready for another shot, if there is one. **second**. If you see that the lob is too deep, turn instantly and run. Make sure that you are running so that when you get to where the ball will be coming down, the ball will land to the side of you so you will be able to execute a forehand shot. You really have to be able to make this shot off the backhand side also, so practice both. As far as any other type of **trick shot or tweener**, know that I believe you should definitely learn how to make a tweener or some variation of a tweener. It is just a fun shot. Get your coach to teach it to you.

Half volleys

If you are going to play tennis in a controlled aggressive manner, then half volleys are shots you must be able to hit with ease. Because you don't want to be backing up when you have to take your opponent's deep balls right after they bounce.

To get a visual for these shots, find a wall. Now throw a ball at the ground right in front of the wall and notice how the ball comes right back off the wall upward toward you. Now to execute the half volley, drop your racket down so that it becomes the wall behind the ball as it is entering the ground. Keep the racket face slightly hooded so as to prevent the ball from going straight up. Do you remember? For every angle, there is an equal and opposite angle. This is what actually takes place. Just make sure that you move your racket forward and up right after contact . . . . I again use Roger Federer as the champion of the half volley. Copy him if you can. Please make a note, if you see Roger Federer move back to hit a ball, you have witnessed a semi-annual event. It is definitely a rarity.

Drop Shots

I save this type of shot for last, as I hope you will do when you play a match. It is a difficult shot at best, and so often it is used when a player gets tight. There are times however when it can definitely be an offensive weapon, especially on a clay or grass court where the bounce will be softer and possibly more irregular. **I will often say to my students that the worst thing that can**

happen when you try a drop shot is that you are successful, because now you think you are good at it, so you start to do more of them. Believe me, they are not shots to go to the bank with. Use them as a change of pace, a surprise, but make sure that you are well inside the baseline before you use this type of shot. Plus you would like to see your opponent somewhere near the back fence. This is another shot to practice. Like any other shot you want to put in your arsenal, practice it over and over. It is really nothing more than a soft slice shot. So to practice it, interchange the drop shot with a slice shot, alternating the two shots. Every time you use this shot in a match. I am sure your coach will be curling his toes, hoping for the best.

Footwork

What transforms a good tennis player into a great tennis player is most always footwork. Great footwork is mandatory to play big tennis. Without great footwork, there are no great tennis players. You must treat footwork as your ticket to success as a tennis player. Be willing to do the work and drilling necessary to call yourself a champion of footwork. If you can't move your feet, the word "golf" comes to mind. **Being able to move your feet with a rhythm that will deliver you to the ball so that you have a smooth momentum going into and through the shot allowing you to finish on**

balance is mandatory. There's no other way to get the job done without great footwork. You must commit to the work that needs to be done to get your feet organized to hit the shot at hand. The only exception is the serve; and even on the serve, immediately after you finish your serve, the feet must get you quickly into position to execute the next shot, "quick feet." You cannot do too many footwork drills. For you to fully develop into a high-level, competitive tennis player, you need to have access to a good physical trainer who is skilled in footwork for tennis. If you play soccer or basketball, you will find those sports to be good cross training for footwork, but there are no footwork drills like the footwork drills that you can do on the court. **Learn to jump rope like a boxer; it is mandatory that you develop this skill. Your jump rope should be the first thing you put**

into your bag and the first thing you take out of your bag when you are training to learn how to organize your feet to execute tennis shots. Jumping rope is mandatory. Jumping rope should be done prior to any workout or tennis match. It is a great way to warm up. Learn some crossover footwork drills, some stutter steps, and sprints on the court. I am sure you know about suicides. Do them till you drop. Mix in your fitness drills with your footwork drills whenever possible. If you run distance, do it on some forgiving surface, i.e., the beach or a treadmill. Your knees don't need the pounding on more cement. Try and find some clay courts to practice on. It will slow the game down and allow you to really work on balanced footwork. Juniors who grow up in countries where they play primarily on clay have a distinct advantage of balanced footwork. I believe that clay is the best court surface for really learning all facets of the game. Playing on a slower surface will allow you to learn the true meaning of balanced footwork. Several years ago, I met a player by the name of Torbin Ulrich, a Davis cup player from Denmark. He had about a twelve-minute video clip of Bjorn Borg from the waist down. Drilling his footwork on clay, no words or music of any kind, only the sound of his feet shuffling about the court. It was amazing to hear the rhythm this shuffling created; the steps were so tiny and quick with the smooth sliding footwork that is associated with clay courts. Torbin had a friend with him named Jeff Borowiak. These two chaps would practice over and over the smooth rhythm of ground strokes **without** a ball, exaggerating the follow-through of their strokes in conjunction with the sound of their breathing. It was almost a form of meditation;

it was at this time that I met a youngster who was a student at Corona del Mar High School in Newport Beach, who also had some really great strokes. He moved beautifully on the court, long hair flowing behind him. His feet also exhibited an extraordinarily smooth rhythm.

His name was Lars Ulrich, Torbin's son. He could never stay very long because he had some drums that needed his full attention. **They were his true passion**, and we all know how that has worked out. I think the band's name is Metallica.

One, two, three split step . . . one, two, three split step—this drill is mandatory for you to learn early in tennis; go up and down the court doing this rhythmical step during your warm-up to help install it solidly into your game. You will find that most all shots will need some semblance of a split step just prior to the execution of the shot, i.e., return of serve, volley, and various forehands. It is a rhythm thing that allows you to move into your shot with a smooth-flowing motion, getting you set just before you hit.

I attended the Davis cup match between the US and Spain in February 2011, when it was played in Austin, Texas.

I wanted to study the footwork of Spain's David Ferrer. I wanted to see how closely it resembled the footwork of Rafa Nadal, also of Spain. I had previously watched Nadal at the Indian Wells tournament in California a year prior. The two are amazingly similar. Both have very quick small steps when moving laterally on the court. In watching Ferrer, I noticed that after he had hit a wide forehand with the use of a simple crossover step, he was able to keep his shuffling feet moving with extremely small quick steps from right to left, while maintaining his feet in a slightly open stance with his left foot facing into the court while his right foot remained aligned with the baseline, allowing him to continue to hit forehands moving from right to left on the court. He would end up hitting a very angled inside-out forehand for a winner without ever hitting one backhand in the entire rally, all forehands; his balance was absolutely perfect. As a result of this type of footwork, Ferrer was able to hit many more forehands than backhands, thus increasing his control of the court with his dominant stroke and allowing him to hit inside-out forehands almost at will. I believe that his ability to run around backhands was the difference in his match with Andy Roddick; hence Spain won the match.

Boxing out of the court with a semi-open stance so that your lead foot is your right foot if you are right handed and vice versa if you are a lefty. This I believe is the desired position for your feet to be in when hitting a forehand. This would mean that your lead foot is pointed in the same direction as the baseline, and your trailing foot is pointed into the court. In this position, you have boxed out the court in front of you. This allows you to move into position to hit the ball when it is in front of you and not to the side of you. Now you are able to fully load your lead foot with your body weight which in turn allows you to push your weight off your loaded foot, in a hip and shoulder rotating motion that will now transfer your body weight onto your lead foot when you follow through and finish. Thus you will be dominating the ball. **There are really**

only two things that can happen regarding you and the ball—either you play the ball or the ball plays you. Nothing really good happens if the ball is continually playing you. Never stop moving your feet so that you are able to get yourself into position behind the ball. Now you are able to really control the ball . . . do something with it! Make it go away.

I believe there are three stances from which you can execute a forehand or a backhand.

1. When you step directly toward the ball in front of you
2. From an open stance.
3. From a closed stance, or stepping across the flight of the ball. If you do hit from a closed stance, allow your trailing foot to swing out into an open stance finish. This will make it easier to return back into the court with a

simple crossover step. This is also should be done for a two-handed backhand, again allowing the trailing foot to swing out into and open stance finish.

In each of these three scenarios, physical balance is easily maintained throughout the completion of the shot.

There are so many professionals that exhibit truly great footwork; however, again Roger Federer is the king. I really can't think of any extended period of time that Federer has been off due to an injury. This I believe is because of his dedication to fitness excellence, which appears to me to begin with footwork. His first step is lightning quick. **It seems to me that your ability to move your feet quickly on balance will pretty much determine the level play you will attain.**

So every time you go on the court to work out, practice, or play a match, have a short conversation with your feet explaining to them in detail just how important it is that they do their job, to the best of their ability. Let them know that you mean business.

Practice

To begin this chapter on practice, I will repeat the often overused phrase, "practice makes perfect." This statement, however, is an unfortunate misnomer. The correct statement should be **practice make permanent**. So make sure you have a great visual of what it is that you want to practice. If it is to become permanent, you want to make sure that it is correct. You certainly don't want to be practicing to become good at doing something incorrectly. My dad once told me, "The only thing that is truly permanent in life is change itself, and in order for there to be progress, there must be change."

However, all change is not positive change, it can also be very negative or destructive, so be careful about what type of change you are accomplishing. Make sure that it is positive change.

Tennis workouts are often filled with different types of court drills, which usually require a student to be running from side to side or up and back or a combination of the two to hit a series of shots. I believe that this type of learning is certainly an asset **if the students can all execute the shots correctly.** Many times, however, the youngsters involved are unable to perform the fundamentals of the shots required, and the tennis drill quickly becomes a sort of a fire drill. Now they are just racing through the shots, never really finishing any of them before taking off for another one; thus, practicing the shots incorrectly and making errors which go uncorrected and sometimes even becoming permanent.

My favorite drill is what I call five-ball. This is a live, one-on-one drill, with the instructor having a basket of balls at his side feeding a ball to the student who in turn has to execute a shot hitting it back to the instructor, who then volleys the ball to a different location on the court and then again the student executes a shot back to the instructor. If the student misses the shot, the instructor feeds out another ball immediately as though the student never missed. This continues until all five balls are gone, then the drill continues with the instructor standing in a different position on the court for every new set of five balls. With this drill, the student is able to focus each time on his fundamental mechanics and begin to perfect shots on the move, each time hitting back to the instructor.

So the player is learning to hit to a certain location from different places on the court.

Here's another good way to learn to execute shots on the move, again using five balls. Each ball is fed to the student who now has to hit to targets that have been strategically placed about the court. Any combination of strokes can be practiced. For example: forehand cross court ground stroke, backhand slice approach shot deep to the backhand side of the court, two closing volleys, and an overhead. These types of drills can be done with up to three students at a time.

For live ball drills with two players hitting off each other's ball, using cross court down the line drills, you need to be sound on your fundamental mechanics so that you are able to control the ball for your drill partner. These are very valuable drills for the advanced player, but if one or both of you can't control the ball, then the drill is nonfunctional, and frustration sets in. If, however, you can execute these types of shots, then this type of drill becomes very valuable because now you can actually compete with each other to see who is first to miss. Now you will be able to find a rhythm to the drill, and you will build confidence in your ability to control the ball and get the ball to do what it is that you want it to do and go where it is that you want it to go. Being able to do this drill means you are a very capable player, and this should be a big sign of accomplishment. **You are improving!**

I watched Jimmy Connors and Michael Pernfors practice prior to the Indian Wells tennis tournament several years ago. There was quite a crowd gathered around the court to watch them practice. When they walked onto the court and were getting ready to rally, I realized that they had only one ball. I couldn't believe it; the ball would go back and forth time after time. They moved each other around the court all the while hitting the same ball without missing. As it turned out, neither one wanted to be the one who missed and had to go and pick up the ball. They were practicing, but they were also competing and performing . . . **When practicing, never miss a chance to compete and perform . . . if not with another person, compete with yourself. Don't miss. The worst miss is a miss in the net.**

I tell that little story so that you as an aspiring tennis player will hate missing when you are practicing; don't tolerate it. Again, compete with the person you are rallying with. You don't want to be the one that misses.

One of my favorite sayings in tennis is "If you want to start Winning . . . stop losing . . . stop missing." Practice with the purpose in mind of making every shot . . . more matches are lost by someone than are won by someone. Remember, winning is only a result of some process, as is losing. Focused practice will increase immensely your chances of getting an "A" or a win on your report card. When you are practicing your strokes, you should be practicing your self-discipline at the same time. Good practice requires strong self-discipline; stay focused on what you are trying to learn. Do it slowly at first so that you can get the feel of what it is that you want to accomplish. My very favorite coach of all time is Coach John Wooden of the UCLA Bruins basketball team. I think his favorite words were "self discipline." I would often go to Pauley Pavilion to watch the Bruins practice; how very precise coach wooden was in directing his players about the court, not only in their execution of drills and plays, but also of their conduct both on and off the court . . . rules for all to abide by . . . self-discipline . . . self-control. All of the players seem to have pride in what they were accomplishing, without all the fine fare, just methodically going about the business of learning and practicing. **They were practicing to achieve excellence by having focused practices—all based in self-discipline**. I learned the phrase **hurry but don't rush** from Coach Wooden. The same is true in tennis . . . hurry but don't rush; stay in control of your actions.

Serving practice

Always practice your serve using targets. It will help you learn to visualize spots on the court. You must be exact in your placement of serves; serving is all about location . . . location. In today's game, using different speeds and spins is almost mandatory to have an effective serve. Be able to interchange your serves, thus keeping your opponent off-balance. Practice your serve with a purpose. Use four or six targets. See how many balls it takes you to knock all the targets down. Again, compete with yourself, then each time you practice your serve, you will have a number to beat. Compete with yourself whenever you can. This will help you to stay mentally focused on just what it is you are doing; **focusing includes visualization. If you can visualize, you can achieve.** Having a visual in serving is so very important. It's the one time you get to hold the ball, so there should absolutely be no outside distractions.

Practice matches

These are a must. These are like quizzes or tests in school. They are a gauge as to your progress. They are rehearsals for tournament matches . . . practice matches are where you will discover at what pace you are improving in shot making—shots you can't get to or shots you can't make today will be shots for you to execute tomorrow. If time is short, play tie breakers. You should be playing some sort of points or games every day . . . this is the only way you can develop your playing skills.

Make sure that you are learning all of the shots in the game. Have a complete game. For sure, know how to serve and volley effectively and how to come in behind an opponent's weak second serve or even first serve. If you can develop this aggressive style of play in practice, you will be comfortable being aggressive in a tournament match. **The practice court is where you learn to make shots, to become a shot maker. This is really where the fun is—making shots, like winners maybe, and you certainly want to practice winners, don't you? Winners, by definition, mean there are no more shots, so hold that finishhhhhh; don't rush the shot**. And the practice match is where you find out if you can actually make the shots you have practiced. If you are not playing at least a couple of practice matches a week, your progress and improvement will be slowed. In order to really become a high-level player, you must in fact play competitive practice matches as often as possible, certainly at least once a week. After each practice or match, ask yourself one question for sure.

Did I test myself today? If the answer is no, then you had a bad tennis day. Striving for excellence means pushing the envelope, demanding more of yourself each and every time you are on the court. Tennis is always played in the now, as in right now. There is no past; there is no future . . . just now. **Can you make the shot right now? Whatever is going to happen depends totally on the shot you are making now. I have been asked, "What is the most important shot in the game?" I always answer that it is the shot you are hitting now, for if you can't make the now shot, then the point is over. You lose**. Making shots is so much fun; missing them, as this new generation says, "Sucks."

When playing practice matches, your goal is to win at least 2 points in a row and don't lose 2 points in a row. Practice playing with controlled aggression. That is being aggressive within a defined space. In other words, you must be able to maintain the center of your core balance when you are in the heat of the battle. Don't outhit your balance . . . Overhitting equals out of control. Sometimes it is even a way of tanking . . . giving up, saying you don't want to hit anymore. Most of the time a bit of anger is involved and that is always disastrous.

Always stay in control of your emotions. Patience is mandatory in a tennis match; you must earn your points. Make sure that you are not backing up when you are hitting a ball. It is okay to back up to get to the ball, but be stepping forward when hitting the ball. Backing up is almost always a negative action. However, today's players are hitting balls deeper and heavier so as to force their opponents to back up more often. So sometimes you will find yourself hitting off your back foot out of necessity. If this does happen, try to make sure that you get the ball back high over the net and deep, with a ton of topspin . . . Also during practice matches, make sure that you are working on giving a good performance . . . like when a singer sings or a musician plays . . . a dress rehearsal . . . a preview of coming attractions. You certainly want to give as good a performance as you can . . . now your pride is involved, show off a bit. Make yourself proud of what you have accomplished. Be willing to place it on display for all to witness. **Make sure you are reacting to the shot you make . . .** for if you are reacting to the shot your opponent makes, you are probably going to be late hitting the ball, and you are on defense. If you are reacting to the shot you have made, it will increase the odds of you being able to act on your opponent's ball, and go on the offense. I am sure you would rather act than react. If you are acting on the ball, you are in control. You are in charge of the point, and you will be able to be more aggressive. It is tough to be aggressive if you are always on defense and reacting to the ball.

Topspin . . . underspin . . . sidespin . . . to be a great player, you must master all types of spins. A spinning ball is a ball under control, and you will be able to execute the type of shot you are wanting to make. The more you learn to spin the ball, the more you are able to control the ball, which will go a long ways toward helping you win the match. When I was coaching David Roditi in Southern California juniors, opposing coaches would tell me, “Your boy has too many weapons.” It was true for sure. In a high school match, I watched David win one point running back for a ball over his head and instead of hitting a tweener, David executed a perfect tweenerlike shot, only from the forehand side of his body with his back facing the net. The execution of the shot was exactly the same as a tweener except it was hit from his right side. The shot rifled past his opponent standing at the net and left him frozen in surprise as the ball shot past him for a winner. Then, a short time later to the absolute amazement of all the folks watching, David made the same shot again, only this time the opponent was ready to volley off the shot when suddenly the ball sailed up and over his head. This time, David executed a perfect lob off exactly the same type of shot. I believe David was sixteen at the time he made these shots, but he had been practicing this shot a long time before. **I say again . . . learn all the shots and have some fun, be a complete player.**

When practicing, make sure you are learning all there is to learn. Being a complete player is so very necessary if you want to play at the level of collegiate competition. There are times when you will find yourself in some deep trouble, you know, way off the court, out of position, and running for your life. This is the time you go for a winner. A career shot! If you miss, you have nothing to lose, but if you were to make it, it would certainly pump you up and probably cause your opponent to think that there is a demon over there! The air might just go out of them . . .

Give it your all when you are practicing. Try for the impossible. Don't quit on a shot.

Once you begin to do that, you will find yourself giving up on balls you might just be able to get to. Your rule should be don't give up on anything. **It is not a habit you should want to develop! When running for a ball that is out of reach, try to at least touch it. Soon you will find that you will be able to actually get to the ball and do something with it. Today's touch is tomorrow's get.**

I believe that you can learn any shot that **you want to learn** . . . Again, how big is your want? Will you invest the necessary time that it takes to learn all the shots? It is more important for you to become a total player, knowing all the shots, than it is to be the number 1 in the 12's. What really counts is being number 1 in the 16's and be totally prepared for higher levels of tennis competition. By the time you are sixteen, you should definitely be playing some 18-level tournaments; even in the 14's you should be playing up into the 16's. Keep your sights set high; keep testing yourself. I was coaching an eighteen-year-old boy in an Austin, Texas, junior tournament in the eighteen and under division. He was playing a boy who was just fourteen. My boy was playing quite well. The score was even about midway through the first set. When suddenly there was a change in the game of the fourteen-year-old. He began to play some pretty outstanding tennis, so the fourteen-year-old won easily at 6 love in the second set. His name was Ryan Harrison. So my boy got a close-up and personal look at a very talented young tennis player. who is now #58 on the ATP pro tennis tour at the age of nineteen and is a member of the United States Davis cup team. He obviously learned all the shots. I feel that sometimes youngsters are pushed so hard to win . . . win . . . win when they are so very young . . . that they never completely learn . . . learn . . . learn . . . then when they get to the higher level of play, they have a tough time competing because they have not learned all of the shots.

Again, become a shot maker—a maker of shots. This is truly where the fun is; winning tennis is making shots, being able to show off a bit, give the folks a great performance. Great players make great shots at tough times. You know like a match point up for you, and you hit a winner. Pride is a powerful feeling. Be proud of yourself and your accomplishments, but always let your racket do the talking. Celebration is good, but not at the expense of anyone else. Make sure that you are always respectful of your opponent and the game of tennis.

Practicing details will make you a more consistent player for sure—**like the detail of watching the ball**. This detail is probably the biggest cause of missing shots even into the professional level. When playing a match or practicing, **you should make sure that your focus is on the watching the ball. You should almost have tunnel vision.** See the ball into your racket on every shot, but then be able to trust your ability enough to keep your head stone-still **and feel the ball go away. Tennis is a game of feelings, not seeings**. If I ask a student about a particular shot he or she had hit, they always say, "It felt really good," or "It didn't feel right." They never say it looked really good. If you want to see the match, I tell the kids to buy a ticket. If you want to feel the match, you can be a player.

Feeling is a much more powerful sense than seeing; players will always say they felt good out there today. I don't think they ever say, "Boy, did I ever look good out there today." The spectator will never have the joy of feeling what you feel.

What you feel and why you feel that way are two important factors for you to understand.

I have often heard players say "I will work it out." To me, that means, "Whatever it is you are working on is already inside of you, and all you have to do is work it out. So when you are practicing, know that the finished product is already in you. Keep on keeping on until you have worked it out." Perseverance is a word that should come to mind when you are practicing. Stay on it . . . over and over . . . with purpose, then you will master it.

Practice visualizing your objectives. Everything starts with a thought. If you can think it, you can visualize it. And if you can visualize it, you can do it. I truly believe that you would not have the passion to play this game of tennis if you didn't have the ability to do it.

The practice court is where mastery and greatness are born; repetition is the mother of all learning. It will make your good motions permanent. Repeat . . . repeat . . . repeat . . . **focus is uninterrupted thought**. If you are practicing to correct a mistake, do it slowly at first until you can feel the correct way to do it. Skill building is confidence building.

It is very important to remember a simple fact: **Mistakes will make you a better player**. They are building blocks for success. If you are not making mistakes, you are pretty much doing nothing because you are not learning. Use practice time efficiently. Don't waste it. Don't play the game trying not to make mistakes. Trying not to do something never works in any endeavor. Let the mistakes happen, then learn how to correct them. **The how to do it is paramount to your growth as a tennis player. Here is where that word "passion" comes in again. You have to love the work in the practice, or you will never be able to truly be a master of your trade.**

If you say you will try . . . not good enough. I know kids who have said they would try, but it was too tough, so they quit trying. There is no commitment in those words. **I will try** never really works out. However, if you say **I will learn it**, you will get it done because your passion will drive you to learn it. **The practice**

court is your office . . . your place where business gets done . . . practice thinking. No nonsense here . . . it is your classroom, your place of learning. If you love the work, don't be distracted by anything. Stay focused and get busy . . . no cell phones, no friends, no distracting factors on the court, nothing to disrupt your thought and . . . focus . . . focus.

Strategy

Whenever you play a competitive match, whether it be a practice match or a tournament match, make sure you have a plan in mind as to how you want to play the match. You should go so far as to write your plan down on some paper so that you can review it during change overs. Keep it simple. When playing practice matches, you must know what it is that you want to accomplish in the match. What are you working on? And don't say everything. You have to be specific; try not to talk in generalities. Or your mind will wander. **Don't just hit balls** and see what happens. Don't worry about winning or losing the match; focus on what you are doing; focus on executing your plan when playing a match. Work on knowing where you want the ball to go . . . have mental targets on the court you want to hit . . . Remember, learning is the most important thing when you are practicing; test yourself to see if you can actually execute the plan you designed. Planning a match requires thinking, and thinking requires focus. This too must be practiced. If you find yourself straying from your plan, bring your focus back to the plan quickly. Keep your thoughts engaged as to what you are doing . . .

I would offer two basic strategic plans. Remember, you are trying to win the match, not keep from losing it; that in itself is a strategy . . . both of these plans require you to be in an aggressive frame of mind; no negativity allowed. **Playing not to lose is never an option**.

Remember, you came to compete . . . not to hope or wish. You should be looking to go on the offense and attack your opponent's weakness. Plan #1: When your opponent gives you a short ball, a ball that lands either on or inside of your service line. This type of ball is wearing a big sign that says "Come on in and attack me."

Plan #2: When you have hit a high heavy ball that lands deep in your opponent's court and is bouncing high and you have them backing up . . . again, there is a big sign. Come on in and enjoy a weak short ball in the middle of your court, so during a baseline rally you should be getting yourself into a position so that one of these two options will take place. **You must recognize both of these options as they are taking place . . . not after they have taken place, then it is too late and you have lost your**

advantage. On both of these plans, go into the court and either hit an outright winner or an approach shot followed with a closing winning volley.

Do all in your power to keep from backing up when you are hitting a ball. I know that sometimes it has to happen, but try and stay in charge of the ball. Again . . . don't let the ball play you.

You play the ball on your terms as it is rising up and full of energy even on the short hop or half volley. Master the ability to hit a half volley from anywhere on the court. This will help to keep you from going too far back; backward is negative. If your opponent is driving you back, then he is coming in, and you don't want that. Now they own the inner part of their court. And you are probably going to lose this particular point. Now for sure we don't want too many second places on points. Every point and every game is a mini match. So you are constantly getting a fresh start many times over in a match. This is what makes tennis so much fun; there is always something new, like a new beginning, a new set of challenges. **You must maintain focus and composure the entire match for however long that takes. Remember, the set you have to win is the last one, not necessarily the first one; however, that is always a good thing to accomplish. Straight-set wins for sure are pretty nifty.**

When standing on your baseline, look to the other side of the court. You will see that it is a rectangle. Now you should be able to visualize that rectangle when you are playing a match. I would like you to believe that those two corners are the money corners. If you are able to consistently get the ball into those two corners, you are going to have to build a bigger trophy case at home. Now that is boiling the cabbage down. This keeps it real simple. Hit deep to the corners . . . now . . . look to the right and left of your baseline. I am pretty sure you will see two corners. Now, **don't let your opponent put the ball in your corners.**

To prevent this from happening, cut your corners off so that your opponent will be playing in a triangle on your side of the court with you being the top of the triangle. When you are practicing and drilling, make sure you keep the ball in front of you so that you can cut off your corners.

Divide your court into three parts: (1) **inside the service line** . . . this is where you need to be when you have the ball and can close the point out. It is not necessarily the place you want to be without the ball. You surely don't want to be close to the net without the ball, or you can start looking up for an overhead coming your way and (2) **between the service line and the baseline** . . . In this the transition area, you should be hitting an approach shot and going in behind it. This area is becoming more and more an area where you hit out right winners, especially topspin swinging volleys off both sides and inside out and inside in forehands off the ground.

Last is the area from (3) **the baseline to the back fence . . .** this is the "jousting" area—the place from where you are working to get yourself into position to make something happen that will provide you with an opening to begin to go into your court and go on the offense. This backcourt area is the area where too many players play too deep. They give away too much court. When you are playing practice matches, use a piece of chalk and draw a line no more than four feet behind the baseline. Do not go behind that line. If your opponent's ball lands deep in your court, stay and learn to hit half volleys rather than back up. You must learn these type of shots to play at the college level of competitive tennis. The further back from the baseline you go, the more you are in negative territory.

If you are able to remain close to the baseline when you are rallying, you might just see an opening where you can hit a shot that will weaken your opponent and put them on the defensive, even get them off-balance, then you can attack from there by trying to hit an outright winner. To illustrate this, think of a boxer. The second he sees he has hit his opponent hard enough to knock him off-balance, he quickly goes in to finish him off because his opponent is in a weakened condition; he is on his heels backing up to regain his balance. **To summarize this, when you are playing a match, be reactive to what you do, not to what your opponent does. For if you are consistently reacting to what your opponent does, you are probably going to come in second again, and I hope that second place is what you had in mind when you started the match.**

An important strategy for you to master is to be able to serve and volley. A major way to practice this phenomenon is playing doubles. I say phenomenon because this type of tennis is slowly becoming a rumor. It is almost nonexistent in women's intercollegiate doubles play. I have watched college level women's doubles play, where one player is up at net and the other is playing a game of singles from the baseline. Somebody never learned to serve and volley or at maybe they are just too afraid to do it, and that is really too bad because the serve and volley game is so much fun to play. I don't want to be picking on the girls, but it seems to be a fact. I would recommend that you again take some chalk and draw a line about three feet behind your service line. This being a guide line for you to use as you practice your split step after you serve. You may be in front of the line or slightly behind the line, after your split step, but it should be close. Now don't just practice your serve. Practice your serve, split step, and volley routine . . . and practice it over and over and over until you own it. **There is only one reason you don't learn to serve and volley, and that is you really don't want to. The important fact must be that you have to want to in order**

to master it. There is that word "want" again. Just how big is your want? Do you really want to learn it badly enough? When you play practice matches, make sure that you develop this ability to serve and volley at strategic times, like on game point even match point. Use it as a surprise, a changeup, something that will get your opponent off-balance. **Sometimes knowing when to do something is also a weapon . . . like for a big serve and volley on your second serve,** especially in the add court coming in behind a big kicker serve so that the return will be weak and you can close with a fine-looking volley winner. Now how nifty would that be? Serving and volleying is such a fun thing to do. Please learn it. You also must be able to go into the court behind your opponent's second serve to get a volley, even behind their first serve if it is weak. Let them know that you came to play, keep looking for opportunities to be aggressive. Make sure that you learn about your opponent in the warm-up. I have had students get halfway through the match before they recognize that their opponent is a lefty. If they are a lefty, then you have to go cross court with more shots to exploit their backhand. See if they have a good slice.

Be aware of what they are doing when they are warming up. Make sure you hit a couple of practice returns when they are practicing their serves.

When the match begins and you win the coin toss, then please choose to serve. **Serving is a positive statement. And it gives you the opportunity to go into the lead; believe in yourself and set the tone for the match; choose to serve.** When you do return serve for the first time, remember to have that little talk with your feet, to get them moving from the get go. Start from a little farther back for their first serve, so you have a little extra time, and then as you get more comfortable, begin to move in more on your return. It is important to remember to have targets on your return of serve. It will get you into the focus mode, and it will jumpstart your thinking mechanism so that you are aware of what you are thinking. **Remember, everything starts with a thought. Make sure they are positive thoughts.** Everything comes from doing . . . be a doer of things . . . not much comes from wishing and hoping; **doing will make you feel good, both in tennis and in life. Do it in a positive way so as to learn and gain confidence. Champions only come from doers. In the musical "The Sound of Music," the words "nothing comes from nothing and**

something comes from something" make you think. How amazingly simple is that? You must do something in order to accomplish something. Set yourself apart from the rest and challenge yourself to go for greatness . . . very few people do.

Fitness

Fitness begins with a commitment to govern what kind of food and drink you are putting in your body. If your wish is to become a high-level player, you must supply your body with the proper high-energy fuel . . . be strict with yourself.

I am not going to recommend any one particular type of food, but I would suggest that you to eat only good carbohydrates . . . prior to a match, no dairy products or fats. They take too long to digest and metabolize; be sure you are completely hydrated well before the match begins, and for sure continue to be drinking all during the match, adding a Gatorade sort of drink to your match intake of fluids is also a good plan. Eat bananas and good energy bars, continue to drink plenty of water or Gatorade after the match; continue to drink more water. If you control the type of fuel you put into your body, your stamina will improve, and you will decrease the chance of cramping during the match. Cramping is match killer.

It is certainly a big asset if you have access to a good fitness trainer. Have him prepare a program for you to follow, with an emphasis on tennis footwork. This will help you to get through two tough matches in the same day and at the same time, train your feet to do what it is you are asking them to do—to move and move quickly with rhythm and balance for an extended period of time. It would be great if you could see your trainer twice a week.

My idea of cross training would be to run some steep hills that have grass on them or at least dirt; run stadium stairs if you have access to them; run suicides on the court until you drop; and then my very favorite is be able to hit one hundred fed balls from side to side the full width of the court from corner to corner with a goal of making at least 90 percent of the shots. When I was coaching David Roditi, he would hit the one hundred balls about twice a week, and if he didn't like the way it went, David would do it again, Sometimes . . . to make sure he left it all out on the court; he would **do the entire basket—that is 250 balls side to side without stopping**. This particular drill should be the last one of the day. I did this with most of my students. I always had someone counting the number of misses, and then I would post the number of misses each time in a notebook. I would make it competitive amongst all my students to see who could get to 100 percent. Over several weeks, I could see not only the improvement in both their fitness and the ease at which they could do the drill, but also the resulting percentage would climb steadily toward the 100 percent level. There are great footwork drills that are done on court that will give you a great fitness workout and at the same time allow you to work on the mechanics of several different types of strokes. The volley, volley, overhead drill is an excellent example. You begin with the feeder hitting you four volleys and then an overhead; first two shots are a swinging topspin forehand volley and a swinging topspin backhand volley, then a normal forehand and backhand volley, then going back for the overhead, then closing to do the same routine over and over for least a set of five. A rest for a minute, then another set of five, and so on . . . until you are maxed out. There are several of these types of drills that will benefit both your practice on correct execution of strokes, plus getting you the footwork practice that is necessary to help quicken your footwork all the while maintaining your physical balance. I will leave it up to you as to other types of on-court fitness drills that you may want to incorporate into your fitness drill session. As a note, to further make these types of on-court drills a test of fitness and balance, do them on a clay court. Now, you are getting it done.

As for running for cardiovascular conditioning and stamina, please run on a forgiving surface—a treadmill, or in the sand, on the beach, or overland. Just stay off concrete. Your joints take enough beating when you are playing your matches on hard courts, but running a few miles a week is certainly a good thing to do. My whole life has been playing athletics on a hard surface, and I now have had four knee surgeries, and I am the proud owner of a metal hip, so be sure to take care of your legs.

Workouts in the weight room have become a must for conditioning. Have your fitness instructor set you up with a weight program. Under fourteen, I would just use your own body weight and resistance exercises. For example: sit-ups, push-ups, etc. Use a lot of isometrics exercises.

Remember to do your fitness after your tennis workouts; for the tennis workouts, you need fresh muscles to be quick and loaded with energy. Sometimes I hear of a student being punished with having to do push-ups while they are doing their tennis workouts.

They're being asked to exhibit a good tennis stroke with the very muscles they have just exhausted doing push-ups. This seems to me to be counterintuitive.

I have always used some sort of attention getting punishment if a student was not performing up to expectations, but I would always hold that until the practice was over. Or to really get their attention, I would dismiss them for the day and ask them to call me when they felt that they would have a better attitude or a willingness to correct whatever their problem was. To reiterate, jumping rope. "You can't do it enough. Turn on some tunes that you like and jump rope to the beat of the music." There are so many tennis players that are also musicians. **Feel the rhythm of the beat and the bounce of the ball, then you will move about the court more in sync with the**

ball. Remember, tennis is all about feeling the ball. What do you do when you hear music? You start to tap your feet. There is something that you feel . . . something inside . . . that is where tennis is really played—inside of you. You have to love the game; true passion comes from deep within; it will drive you to the very places you dream about.

You don't want your mind making appointments your body can't keep, so make sure you dedicate yourself to doing the work that it takes to get you where you want to go. No excuses; you have to pay the price. Determination and perseverance are words to embrace in order for you to go out on the court for a tennis match and know that you are ready to compete.

Summary

In summarizing the information in this book, I will outline just how difficult it is to become a complete tennis player..a player of excellence. You will see how each category not only relates to, but also depends upon all of the other categories for you to achieve excellence. The game is like a giant puzzle, if even one category is missing, then tennis excellence is almost impossible to achieve. So you must commit to achieving excellence in each and every category.

First and foremost, you must understand that the mental aspect of the game will pretty much control the physical aspect of your game. The mind definitely rules the body!!

You must be able to control what you are thinking about when you are practicing or competing in a match. Positive thinking is mandatory!!

All ground strokes are totally dependent on the serve and the service return. For if they are not successful, you will not be needing any of your beautiful ground strokes you have worked so hard to master. So if you make the serve and the service return the centerpieces of your game, then you can continue to play.

For any of the above to have a chance for success, your footwork becomes a really big deal. Footwork excellence is mandatory!! For if you are unable to get to where you need to be, you will not be able to exhibit that great shot you need to make to win the point.

Next, you must rigorously practice all of the pieces to your game on the practice court. The practice court is also where you learn to develop strategies or plans so that you can turn your game into a winning game.

Lastly, you must achieve fitness excellence, in order to finish two tough three setters in the same day.

Having completed all of the work necessary to achieve excellence in each of the aforementioned categories, you are ready to compete at the intercollegiate level of tennis. After that, what else is there? For there to be anything else, it will depend entirely on what more you want to do.

Addendum

Dear junior tennis player,

I am sure that you will find some repetition of information in this book. Know that there are some things that are important enough to be repeated. Like loving the practice time—it's necessary to practice, practice, practice.

Excellence in tennis or any other endeavor begins with the words **I want to be.** I ask you now, just what do you want to be and how badly do you want it? This is a powerful question.

The words I want to be are a really big deal if you truly mean what you say. So many of the words you use—such as I hope or I wish—are words for birthday candles and for things that you can't control. Replace them with the words **I want to achieve tennis excellence.** Your destiny does not depend on what other people say or think, because you and you alone control your destiny. It is all about you and what you think and what you want to be. If you really want to be an accomplished tennis player, it is all up to you, and what you are willing to sacrifice to reach your goal. **Don't let anything come between you and what you want. Remember, you are one of a kind, someone really special, no duplications or carbon copies . . . only you.**

You will never get to where you want to go, unless you start, so why not start now? Though it is tough to start, once underway that passion you have inside of you will supply you with the necessary drive and direction to achieve the tennis excellence you seek to attain. **I truly believe that you would not have this passion for tennis**

excellence if God had not blessed you with the talent for the game.

So for all you juniors who have already started your journey toward tennis excellence, look inside yourself and make sure **that you can say this out loud:**

I want to earn the right to be able to compete at the intercollegiate level of tennis, and I am willing to do whatever is necessary to get there. Nothing will detour me.

As they say in the army, be all you can be at whatever it is that you want to be. Stand tall and be proud of all you are accomplishing. Remember, **pride and self-respect are earned, not given.**

Congratulations to all who accept the challenge to venture forth toward tennis excellence. Good luck!

Bob Clauson

CPSIA information can be obtained
at www.ICGtesting.com
Printed in the USA
BVHW030742270120
570595BV00002B/4/J